Quick and easy yoga ideas for every month of the year

Monthly Kids Yoga Themes

BY GISELLE SHARDLOW

Copyright © 2018 by Giselle Shardlow
Cover and yoga pose illustrations by Michael Koch
All images © 2018 Giselle Shardlow

All rights reserved. No part of this book may be reproduced in any form by any electronic or mechanical means, including photocopying, recording, or information storage and retrieval without written permission from the author. The author, illustrator, and publisher accept no responsibility or liability for any injuries or losses that may result from practicing the yoga poses outlined in this book. Please ensure your own safety and the safety of the children.

ISBN: 978-1-943648-26-9

Kids Yoga Stories
Boston, MA
www.kidsyogastories.com
www.amazon.com/author/giselleshardlow

Email us at info@kidsyogastories.com.

What do you think? Let us know what you think of *Monthly Kids Yoga Themes* at feedback@kidsyogastories.com.

WELCOME TO MONTHLY KIDS YOGA THEMES

Are you looking for easy kids yoga ideas?

This book is for primary school teachers, kids yoga teachers, parents, caregivers, health practitioners, and recreation staff looking for simple, convenient ways to add yoga into their curriculum, classes, or home life.

To spark your imagination, each monthly theme includes:

- One breathing technique
- One focus yoga pose
- A three-pose flow sequence
- One focus yoga book

Each theme offers an opportunity to learn about a topic through movement. These yoga themes are designed for children ages three to eight, but they could be adapted for younger or older children. Many of the topics are common in standard preschool and kindergarten classroom curriculums.

Each session can last between fifteen and forty-five minutes, depending on the needs and requirements of the children participating. In preparation for your monthly thematic yoga experience, feel free to gather props and information on that topic. Use resources such as YouTube clips, newspaper articles, magazine pictures, old calendar pictures, Internet sites, guest speakers, brochures, and fiction and non-fiction books to expand the lesson as you see fit.

To make your monthly yoga experience as successful as possible:

- Focus on having fun with movement, not on practicing perfectly aligned poses.
- Engage the children.
- Follow their passions and interests.
- Create authentic, meaningful experiences.
- Cater to their energy levels and different learning styles.

- Be creative and enjoy yourself—the kids will notice your enthusiasm.
- Wear comfortable clothing and practice barefoot.
- Safety is top priority. Clear the space of obstacles and be safe with your bodies.
- Encourage the children to share their yoga experiences with their families and friends.
- Use the kids yoga ideas in this book as a springboard and add other age-appropriate theme-related yoga poses, breathing techniques, relaxation stories, or meditations.

Get children learning, moving, and having fun with these quick and easy monthly yoga themes!

TABLE OF CONTENTS

JANUARY   Winter Yoga. 1

FEBRUARY   Love Yoga 5

MARCH   Spring Yoga 9

APRIL   Earth Yoga 13

MAY   Animal Yoga. 17

JUNE   Summer Yoga 21

JULY   Rainforest Yoga 25

AUGUST   Beach Yoga 29

SEPTEMBER Fall Yoga 33

OCTOBER   Farm Yoga 37

NOVEMBER   Gratitude Yoga. 41

DECEMBER   Kindness Yoga 45

JANUARY

WINTER YOGA

Focus Breath

Power Breath

Focus Yoga Pose

Warrior 2 Pose

Focus Yoga Flow

Warrior 2 Pose

Warrior 3 Pose

Downhill Skier Pose

Focus Yoga Book

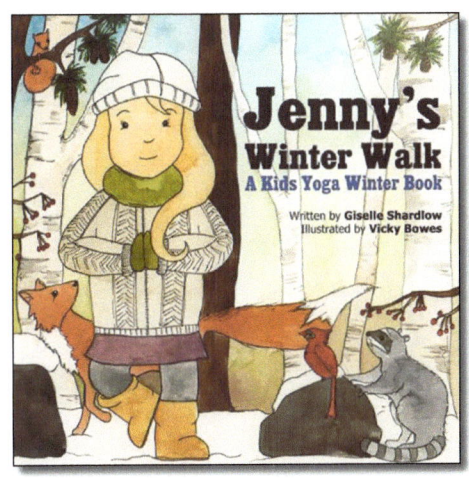

JANUARY

WINTER YOGA
FOCUS BREATH:
Power Breath

Choose a standing or comfortable upright position such as sitting in a chair, sitting cross-legged, or sitting on your heels.

Take a deep breath in through your nostrils for three counts while raising both of your arms above your head. Clench your hands into fists, then exhale vigorously through your mouth and say, "Ha!" At the same time, bring your fists quickly to your chest.

You could also practice this technique doing one arm at a time. Think of pulling the power of the winter sun into your body through your chest. Repeat this breathing technique a few times to bring warmth to your body.

Find this Power Breath technique in the Yoga4Classrooms Card Pack.

KIDS YOGA STORIES™
Learn. • Be Active. • Have Fun.

WINTER YOGA

FOCUS YOGA FLOW:
Warrior 2 Pose, Warrior 3 Pose, and Downhill Skier Pose

JANUARY

WARRIOR 2 POSE
Pretend to be a snowboarder.
From standing position, step one foot back, placing the foot so that it is facing slightly outward. Take your arms up until they are parallel to the ground, in the same direction as your legs. Roll your shoulders back to open your chest, bend your front knee, and look forward. Pretend to cruise down the mountain on a snowboard.

WARRIOR 3 POSE
Pretend to be an ice skater.
Stand on one leg. Extend the other leg behind you, flexing your foot. Bend your torso forward and take your arms out and back alongside your body. Imagine gliding on the ice like a skater.

DOWNHILL SKIER POSE
Pretend to be a downhill skier.
Stand tall with your arms at your sides and your feet hip-width apart. This is Mountain Pose. From Mountain Pose, bend your knees and lean forward to rest your elbows on your thighs, slightly above your knees. Clasp your hands together, keep a straight spine, and look forward. Pretend to ski down the mountain.

KIDS YOGA STORIES™
Learn. • Be Active. • Have Fun.

JANUARY

WINTER YOGA
FOCUS YOGA BOOK:
Jenny's Winter Walk

Join Jenny as she meets various animals while on a winter walk with her mom. Be a squirrel, a fox, and a bunny. Discover winter, explore movement, and learn the five senses.

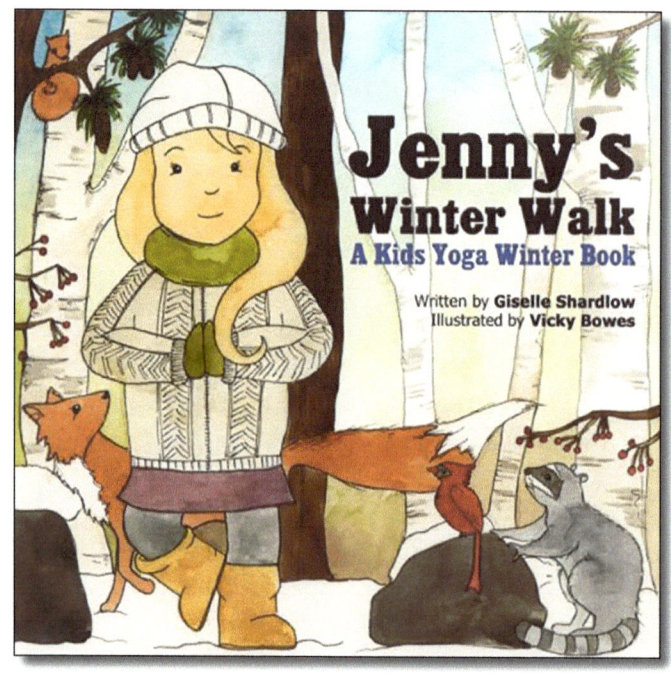

KIDS YOGA STORIES™
Learn. • Be Active. • Have Fun.

FEBRUARY

LOVE YOGA

Focus Breath

Loving Kindness Breath

Focus Yoga Pose

Cobra Pose

Focus Yoga Flow

Table Top Pose

Cobra Pose

Child's Pose

Focus Yoga Book

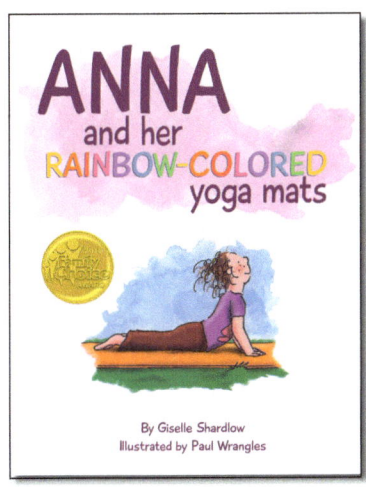

FEBRUARY

LOVE YOGA
FOCUS BREATH:
Loving Kindness Breath

Choose a standing or comfortable upright position such as sitting in a chair, sitting cross-legged, or sitting on your heels. Close your eyes if that is comfortable and begin to tune in to the sound of your breath. Then take a deep breath in and slowly exhale for five counts.

On your next exhale, think of filling yourself with love. Imagine the color red enveloping your body.

On the next exhale, think of sending love and kindness to someone close to you. Then as you exhale, send loving kindness to someone you are having a difficult relationship with at the moment.

Then send love and kindness out to the world around you, the animals, the trees, your neighbors, and your city.

Lastly, send out love and kindness to the world. Finish your loving kindness breath by coming back to breathing naturally. When you are ready, open your eyes.

KIDS YOGA STORIES™
Learn. • Be Active. • Have Fun.

LOVE YOGA

FOCUS YOGA FLOW:
Table Top Pose, Cobra Pose, and Child's Pose

FEBRUARY

TABLE TOP POSE
Stabilize your spine.

Come to an all-fours position with your fingers spread out and palms flat on the ground. Ensure that your back and neck are in a straight but neutral position. Your shoulders should be over your wrists, and your hips should be over your knees. The tops of your feet are flat on the ground.

COBRA POSE
Heart-opening posture.

Lie on your tummy with your legs straight out behind you. Activate your leg muscles by pressing your thighs and the tops of your feet against the ground. Place your palms flat next to your shoulders and draw your shoulder blades together down your back. Press into your hands and gently lift your head, chest, and shoulders off ground as you inhale. Then exhale deeply. Coming even just a few inches off the ground is perfect. Think of your heart opening up to receiving love. Take a few deep breaths. Then as you exhale, slowly bring your forehead back to the ground and allow your lower back to relax.

CHILD'S POSE
Resting position.

Sit on your heels, slowly bring your forehead down to rest in front of your knees, rest your arms down alongside your body, and take a few deep breaths. Think of how you give your love to others. Think of feeling safe and secure.

KIDS YOGA STORIES™
Learn. • Be Active. • Have Fun.

FEBRUARY

LOVE YOGA

FOCUS YOGA BOOK:
Anna and her Rainbow-Colored Yoga Mats

Anna finds happiness practicing yoga on her rainbow-colored yoga mats at recess. She imagines traveling the world and exploring new places. Experience the benefits of yoga with your children or students by acting out this story or discussing what it means to be happy. This book is available in English, Portuguese, Spanish, and French.

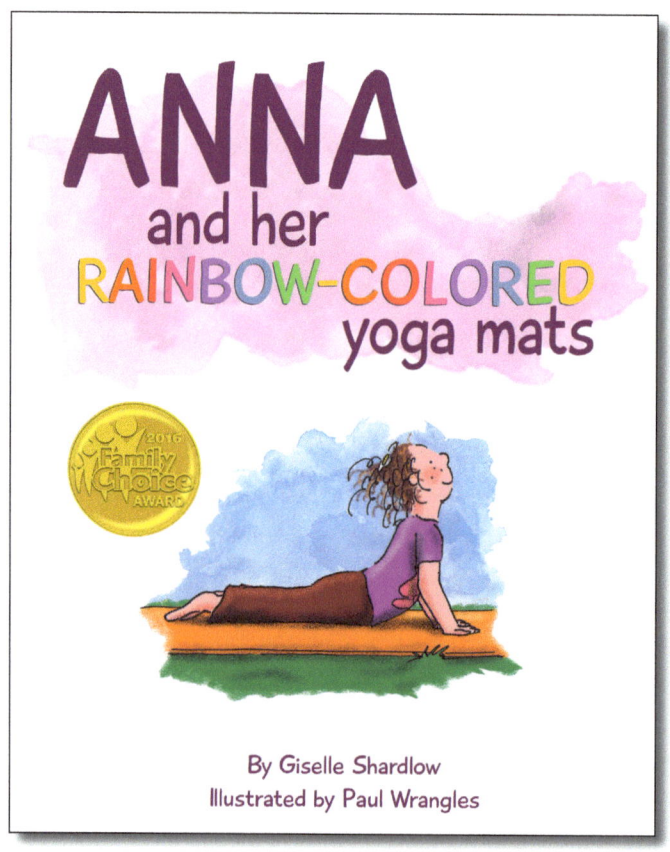

KIDS YOGA STORIES™
Learn. • Be Active. • Have Fun.

SPRING YOGA

MARCH

Focus Breath

Flower Breath

Focus Yoga Pose

Cobbler's Pose

Focus Yoga Flow

Hero Pose

Cobbler's Pose

Flower Pose

Focus Yoga Book

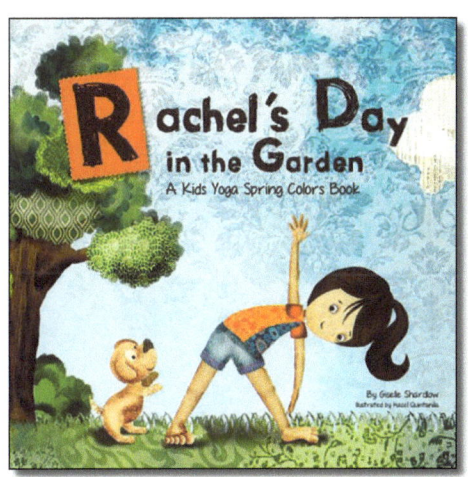

MARCH

SPRING YOGA
FOCUS BREATH:
Flower Breath

Choose a standing or comfortable upright sitting position such as sitting in a chair, sitting cross-legged, or sitting on your heels. Close your eyes, if that is comfortable, and begin to tune in to the sound of your breath.

Imagine you are holding a flower. Imagine the color and smell of that flower. Then take in a deep breath, pretending to smell that flower. Exhale naturally.

Repeat the cycle of a strong inhale and gentle exhale for a couple of minutes, if possible.

You could pretend to smell a different flower each time you inhale. You could also imagine yourself sitting in a meadow of fresh flowers.

This flower breath is an easy way to help children become aware of their breath.

KIDS YOGA STORIES™
Learn. • Be Active. • Have Fun.

SPRING YOGA

FOCUS YOGA FLOW:
Hero Pose, Cobbler's Pose, and Flower Pose

MARCH

HERO POSE
Pretend to be a bee.
Come down to sit upright on your heels, buzz with your arms, and practice a humming breath. Pretend to buzz around the garden like a bee.

COBBLER'S POSE
Pretend to be a butterfly.
Come to sit on your buttocks with a tall spine, bend your legs, and place the soles of your feet together. Place your index fingers above your head like the butterfly's antenna and gently flap your legs like the wings of a butterfly.

FLOWER POSE
Pretend to be a flower.
While in Cobbler's Pose, inhale and tighten you belly as you lift your legs. Balance on your sitting bones, and weave your arms under your legs. Lift your chest, squeeze your shoulder blades together, and ensure that your spine is straight. Hold your arms steady under your legs, with your palms facing up (or in a gyan mudra). Pretend to blossom like a flower.

KIDS YOGA STORIES™
Learn. • Be Active. • Have Fun.

MARCH

SPRING YOGA

FOCUS YOGA BOOK:
Rachel's Day in the Garden

Act out a day in the garden with Rachel. Join her as she and her puppy, Sammy, look for signs of spring. Crawl like a caterpillar, buzz like a bee, and flutter like a butterfly. Discover spring, explore movement, and learn the colors of the rainbow. This award-winning book is perfect for toddlers and preschoolers, ages two to five.

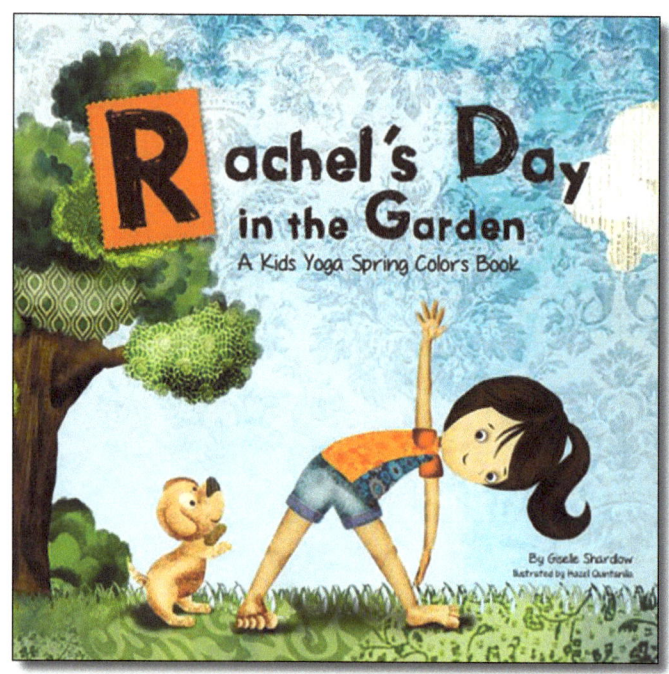

KIDS YOGA STORIES™
Learn. • Be Active. • Have Fun.

APRIL

EARTH YOGA

Focus Breath

Woodchopper Breath

Focus Yoga Pose

Squat Pose

Focus Yoga Flow

Squat Pose

Tree Pose

Extended Mountain Pose

Focus Yoga Book

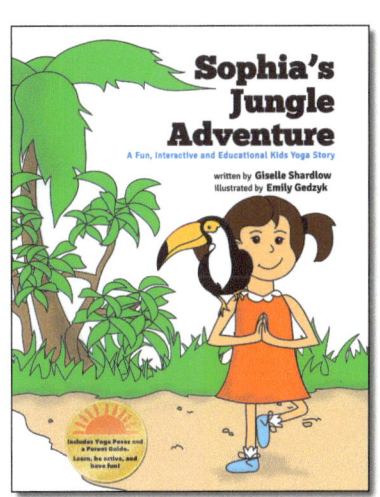

APRIL

EARTH YOGA
FOCUS BREATH:
Woodchopper Breath

Stand tall in Mountain Pose and take a few deep breaths. Then take your feet mat-width apart. Clasp your hands together in front of your body.

Take a long breath in while raising your hands above your head, and then on a vigorous exhale with your mouth open, forcefully take your hands down between your legs. Hang your head and completely let go of all the tension in your body.

Close your eyes, if that feels comfortable, and repeat the steps: long exhale with hands overhead, followed by vigorous exhale and hands down between your legs.

Pretend to be a woodchopper cutting a log for a campfire. Repeat this breathing technique a few times, allowing the children to find their own rhythm and become aware of their breath.

Stand tall in Mountain Pose again and come back to breathing naturally. Let the children feel the effects of this energizing breath technique.

KIDS YOGA STORIES™
Learn. • Be Active. • Have Fun.

EARTH YOGA

FOCUS YOGA FLOW:
Squat Pose, Tree Pose, and Extended Mountain Pose

APRIL

SQUAT POSE
Pretend to be a seed.
Stand tall in Mountain Pose with your toes touching and ankles slightly apart. Then bend your legs to come to a squat position with your knees and toes together. You could take your hands in front of your heart as if you are in prayer then take them to the ground for balance. Your heels will most likely be off the ground, depending on your flexibility. Drop your head and round your back. Pretend to be a seed about to sprout.

TREE POSE
Pretend to be a tree.
From Squat Pose, come up slowly to a standing position. Shift to standing on one leg, bend the knee of your free leg, place the sole of your foot on the inner thigh of your standing leg, and balance. Sway like a tree.

EXTENDED MOUNTAIN POSE
Say hello to the sun.
Stand tall in Mountain Pose and, on an inhale, take your arms up over head to the sky. Look up and say hello to the sun. Exhale and bring your arms back along your sides.

KIDS YOGA STORIES™
Learn. • Be Active. • Have Fun.

APRIL

EARTH YOGA
FOCUS YOGA BOOK:
Sophia's Jungle Adventure

Join Sophia on a jungle adventure. Fly like a toucan, slither like a snake, and flutter like a butterfly as you act out this journey through a Costa Rican jungle. The storybook includes a list of kids yoga poses and a parent-teacher guide. This yoga book for ages three to seven is more than a storybook—it's also a unique experience for children. *Sophia's Jungle Adventure* is also available in Spanish, French, Italian, Portuguese, Russian, German, and Chinese. To extend your child's learning, check out the matching *Sophia's Jungle Adventure Yoga Cards* and *Sophia's Jungle Adventure Coloring Book*.

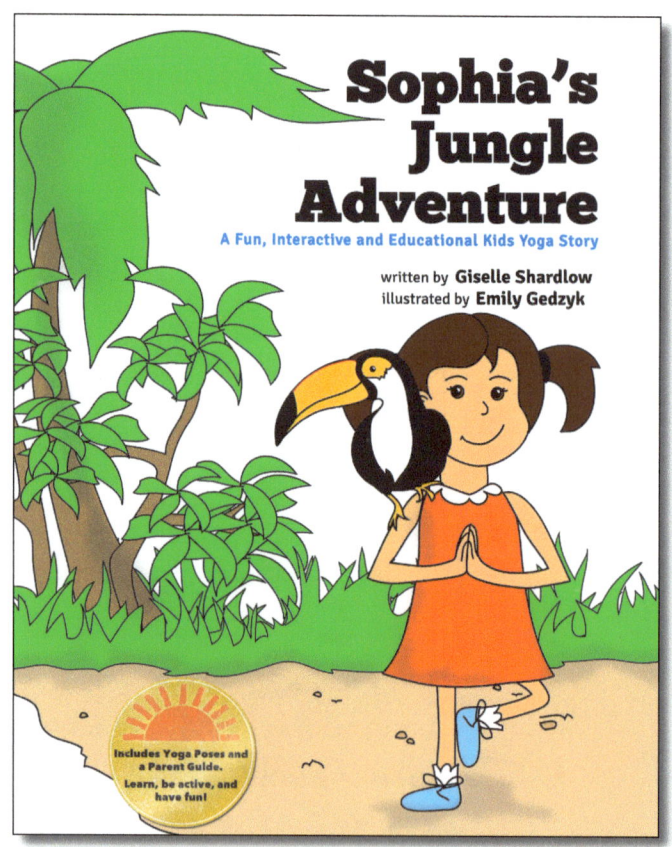

ANIMAL YOGA

MAY

Focus Breath

Lion's Breath

Focus Yoga Pose

Cat Pose

Focus Yoga Flow

Downward-Facing Dog Pose

Cat Pose

Extended Child's Pose

Focus Yoga Book

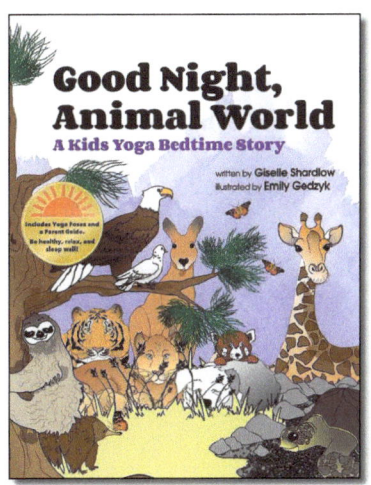

MAY

ANIMAL YOGA

FOCUS BREATH:
Lion's Breath

Come to an all-fours position (or Hero Pose). Take a few breaths to neutralize your spine. Then take a deep breath in through your nose.

As you exhale, look forward and simultaneously open your mouth, stick out your tongue, and exhale audibly, making a "ha" sound.

Breathe in through your nose and repeat the steps, ending by exhaling through your mouth with your tongue out, pretending to be a lion.

Repeat the lion's breath a few times while it feels comfortable, then come back to an all-fours position and breathe naturally.

Lion's breath is an energizing breath technique that's great for teaching children to build breath awareness.

KIDS YOGA STORIES™
Learn. • Be Active. • Have Fun.

ANIMAL YOGA

FOCUS YOGA FLOW:
Downward-Facing Dog Pose, Cat Pose, and Extended Child's Pose

MAY

DOWNWARD-FACING DOG POSE
Pretend to be a sheepdog.
Come down to your hands and feet, with your buttocks up in the air in an upside-down V shape. Ensure your spine is straight and your palms are flat. Stretch and bark like a sheepdog.

CAT POSE
Pretend to be an African lion.
Shift forward and drop your knees to an all-fours position. Spread your fingers. Check that your shoulders and elbows are directly over your hands and that your hips are directly over your knees. Your back should be flat, and your neck should be in a neutral position while you look down at the floor. On an exhale, gently drop your head, press your tummy up, round your spine, and tuck in your tailbone. Look forward for a lion's breath.

EXTENDED CHILD'S POSE
Pretend to be a turtle.
Drop your buttocks to your heels, slowly bring your forehead down to rest in front of your knees, and reach your arms out in front of you. Place the palms of your hands flat on the floor. Take a few deep breaths. Pretend to be a sea turtle.

KIDS YOGA STORIES™
Learn. • Be Active. • Have Fun.

MAY

ANIMAL YOGA

FOCUS YOGA BOOK:
Good Night, Animal World

Help your children sleep better with this yoga bedtime story for toddlers and preschoolers. Say good night to the animals of the world through calming yoga poses for kids. Join six yoga kids as you perch like a bald eagle, crouch like a tiger, and curl up like a sloth. Included is a list of yoga poses and a parent guide with tips on creating a successful bedtime experience. The book is suitable for ages two to five. Try the matching *Good Night, Animal World Yoga Cards* for creative and independent play.

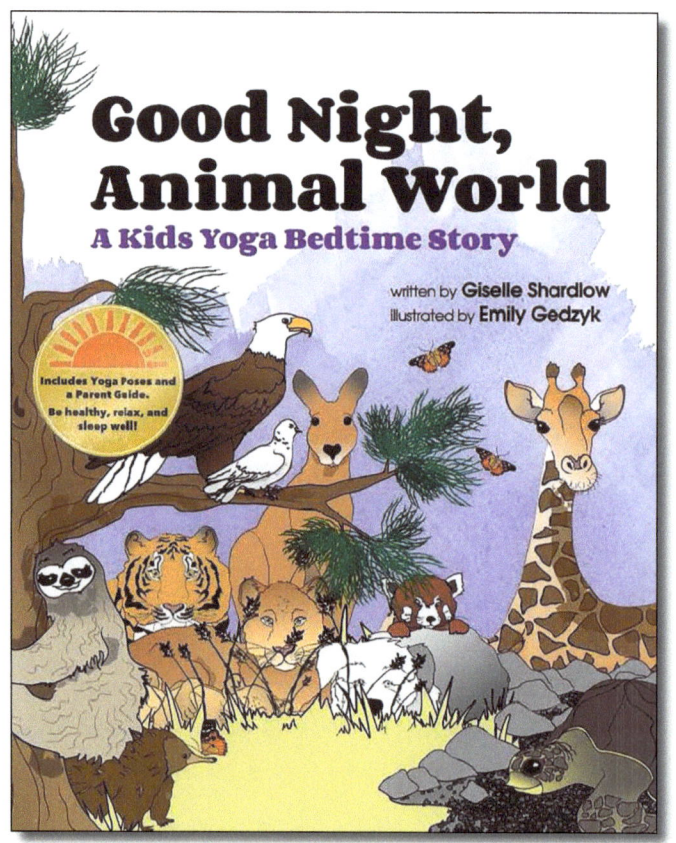

KIDS YOGA STORIES™
Learn. • Be Active. • Have Fun.

JUNE

SUMMER YOGA

Focus Breath

Cooling Breath

Focus Yoga Pose

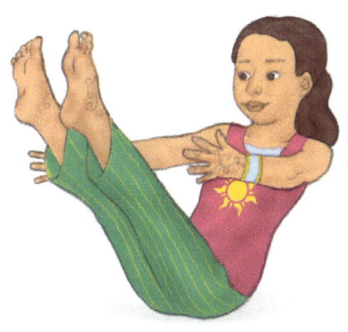

Boat Pose

Focus Yoga Flow

Triangle Pose

Plank Pose

Boat Pose

Focus Yoga Book

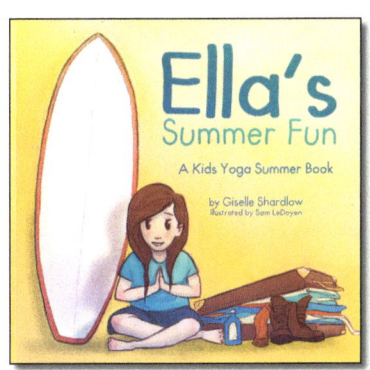

JUNE

SUMMER YOGA

FOCUS BREATH:
Cooling Breath

The cooling breath is great for calming and cooling your body.

Come to sitting comfortably on a chair or a cushion with your hands in your lap and your spine straight. Take a few breaths to calm your mind and body.

Come to the present moment. When you are ready, curl your tongue lengthwise, as if your tongue is a hot dog bun wrapping around a hot dog.

Inhale gently through your mouth, feeling the breath cool your tongue. Then close your mouth and exhale through your nose.

Repeat this a few times to get the hang of it and then return to breathing normally.

KIDS YOGA STORIES™
Learn. • Be Active. • Have Fun.

SUMMER YOGA

FOCUS YOGA FLOW:
Triangle Pose, Plank Pose, and Boat Pose

JUNE

TRIANGLE POSE
Pretend to be a sailboat.
From Mountain Pose, step one foot back, placing the foot facing slightly outward. Take your arms up parallel to the ground then bend at your waist, tilting your upper body. Reach your front hand to gently rest on your shin and reach your other arm straight up. Pretend to be a sailboat cruising along the water. Repeat the steps on the other side.

PLANK POSE
Pretend to be a surfboard.
From Triangle Pose, slide the hand on your shin to the ground while pulling your raised arm down. Place both palms flat on the ground in front of your front foot. As if you are about to do a push-up, step both feet back so that you are balanced on your palms and on your bent toes, keeping your arms straight and your back long and flat. Pretend to be a surfboard gliding through the water.

BOAT POSE
Pretend to be a boat.
From Plank Pose, step your feet forward and come to sit sitting with a tall spine and your legs bent. Lean back slightly, take your arms straight out parallel in front of you, balance on your buttocks, and lift your straightened legs to forty-five degree angle in front of you. Ensure that your spine is straight, your chest is open, and your shoulder blades are pressed together. Then rock in the water like a boat.

KIDS YOGA STORIES™
Learn. • Be Active. • Have Fun.

JUNE

SUMMER YOGA

FOCUS YOGA BOOK:
Ella's Summer Fun

Act out your favorite summer activities with Ella as she experiences a week full of fun summer activities with her grandparents. Be a surfer, water skier, and swimmer. Discover summer, explore movement, and learn the days of the week! Age group: Preschoolers, ages three to six.

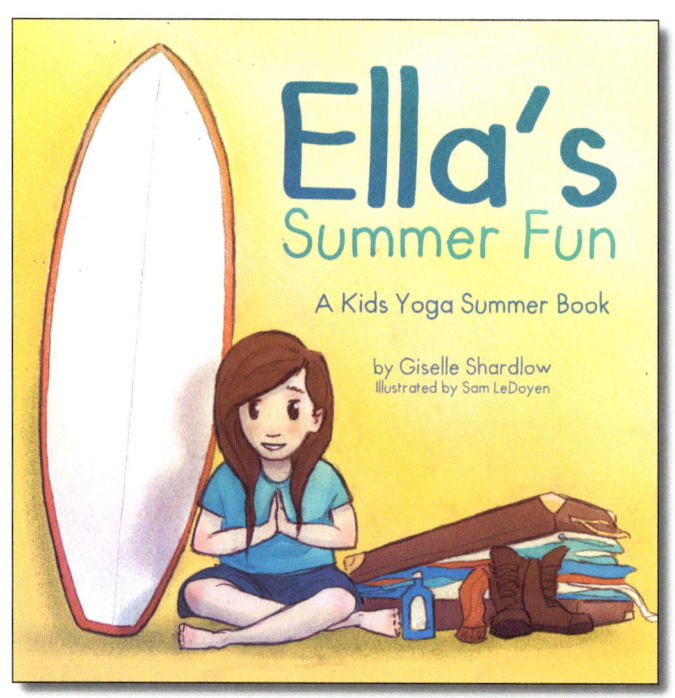

KIDS YOGA STORIES™
Learn. • Be Active. • Have Fun.

RAINFOREST YOGA

JULY

Focus Breath

Mindful Breath

Focus Yoga Pose

Standing Forward Bend

Focus Yoga Flow

Warrior 3 Pose

Standing Forward Bend

Squat Pose

Focus Yoga Book

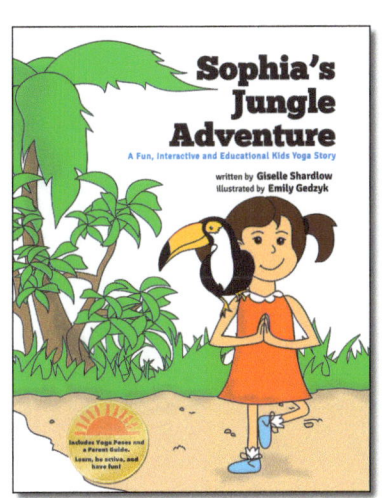

JULY

RAINFOREST YOGA

FOCUS BREATH:
Mindful Breath

Come to sitting comfortably on a chair or a cushion with your palms resting on your knees and your spine straight. Take a few breaths to calm your mind and body. Come to the present moment.

When you are ready, take a three-count inhale followed by a three-count exhale. Once you have the rhythm of your mindful breathing, start to imagine the sounds you might hear in the rainforest.

Think of frogs croaking, birds singing, monkeys howling, snakes hissing, and rain falling. You could also play rainforest sounds in the background to help you imagine sitting in the middle of a rainforest. Imagine the smells of the rainforest and feel the humid heat on your body.

Continue with this mindful breathing technique for a few minutes, as long as it feels comfortable to you.

KIDS YOGA STORIES™

Learn. • Be Active. • Have Fun.

RAINFOREST YOGA

FOCUS YOGA FLOW:
Warrior 3 Pose, Standing Forward Bend, and Squat Pose

JULY

WARRIOR 3 POSE
Pretend to be a toucan.
Stand on one leg. Extend the other leg behind you. Bend your torso forward and take your arms out to the sides. Flap your arms like the wings of the toucan.

STANDING FORWARD BEND
Pretend to be a waterfall.
Come to standing tall in Mountain Pose with your feet hip-width apart and your arms by your side. Slowly bend your upper body, let your arms hang heavy, and reach for your toes. Imagine that your upper body is the rushing water of a waterfall. Take a few deep breaths and relax your body. Close your eyes, if that feels okay. Keep your knees slightly bent to ease the tension in your back. Allow your mind and body to rest. When you're ready, on an inhale, slowly come up to standing by rolling up your back, one vertebrate at a time. Return to standing in Mountain Pose.

SQUAT POSE
Pretend to be a monkey.
Come down to a squat and tap your chest like a monkey.

KIDS YOGA STORIES™
Learn. • Be Active. • Have Fun.

JULY

RAINFOREST YOGA

FOCUS YOGA BOOK:
Sophia's Jungle Adventure

Sophia and her family act out what they see and hear on their hike through the jungles of Costa Rica. Readers fly like a toucan, slither like a snake, and flutter like a butterfly. The *Sophia's Jungle Adventure* Yoga Cards extend your child's jungle yoga adventure and offer another opportunity for creative, independent play. Children can sort the poses or match the poses to the jungle-themed keyword cards. This book is also available in seven other languages: Spanish, Portuguese, French, Chinese, Russian, Italian, and German.

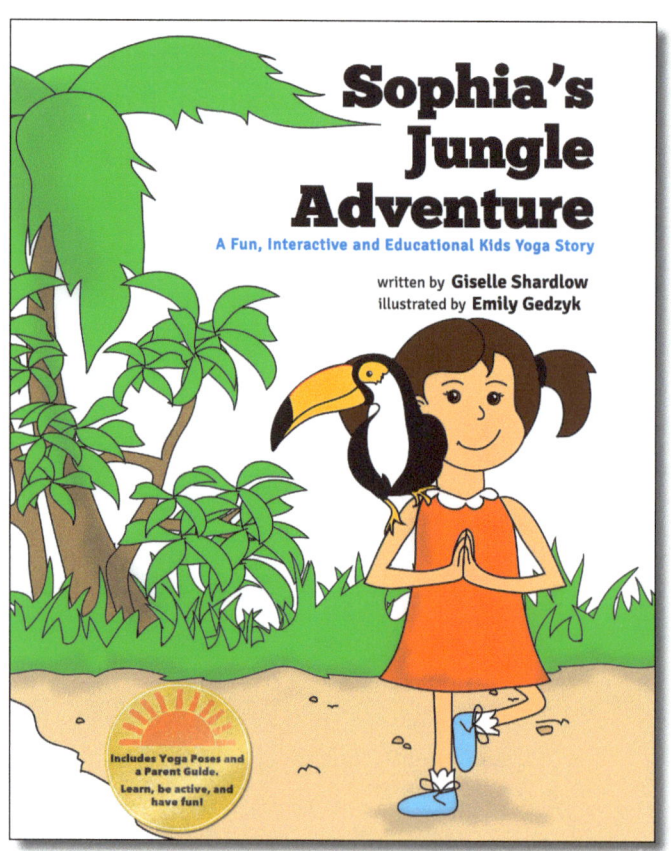

KIDS YOGA STORIES™
Learn. • Be Active. • Have Fun.

AUGUST

BEACH YOGA

Focus Breath

Ocean Breath

Focus Yoga Pose

Downward-Facing Dog Pose

Focus Yoga Flow

Downward-Facing Dog Pose

Pigeon Pose

Hero Pose

Focus Yoga Book

AUGUST

BEACH YOGA

FOCUS BREATH:
Ocean Breath

Ocean breath is associated with practicing vinyasa yoga, when we link movement to breath. In yoga class, we commonly refer to ocean breath as our "ujjayi breath." This translates as "victorious breath" in Sanskrit.

To practice ocean breath, come to sitting or standing comfortably. Close your eyes, if that feels comfortable, or gaze gently down in front of you. Take a few deep breaths to calm your mind and body. Come to the present moment. Breathe in and out through your nose with your mouth closed.

The next time you exhale, make an audible sound in the back of your throat. Exhale audibly for a count of three, followed by an inhale for another count of three. Think of making ocean sounds with your breath. Turn inward and imagine sitting on the beach, listening to the waves crashing on the beach. Continue with this three-count breath for a few minutes. When you are ready, open your eyes and breathe naturally.

BEACH YOGA

FOCUS YOGA FLOW:
Downward-Facing Dog Pose, Pigeon Pose, and Hero Pose

AUGUST

DOWNWARD-FACING DOG POSE
Pretend to be a sandcastle.
From a standing position, bend down and place your palms flat on the ground. Spread your fingers and press your palms flat onto the floor. Step your feet back to create an upside-down V shape with your buttocks high in the air. Straighten your legs, sending your heels gently to the ground. Relax your head and neck and look down between your legs. Think of squeezing your shoulder blades together, creating space between your shoulders and your ears. Imagine being a sandcastle.

PIGEON POSE
Pretend to be a seagull.
From Downward-Facing Dog Pose, bring your right knee to rest behind your right hand, placing your right foot slightly inwards. Perch like a seagull. Repeat the steps on the other side.

HERO POSE
Pretend to listen to sounds of the ocean.
Step your right foot back and rest upright on your heels. Place your palms on your knees. Imagine listening to the waves crashing on the beach. Try practicing your ocean breath.

KIDS YOGA STORIES™
Learn. • Be Active. • Have Fun.

AUGUST

BEACH YOGA

FOCUS YOGA BOOK:
Luke's Beach Day

This story follows Luke and his classmates on a class trip to the beach. Readers act out what the students see and hear, hopping like a kangaroo, perching like a sea gull, and resting like a sea star. Luke's day inspires him to be more conscious of the environment around him.

KIDS YOGA STORIES™
Learn. • Be Active. • Have Fun.

SEPTEMBER

FALL YOGA

Focus Breath

Flying Bird Breath

Focus Yoga Pose

Warrior 3 Pose

Focus Yoga Flow

Warrior 3 Pose

Squat Pose

Child's Pose

Focus Yoga Book

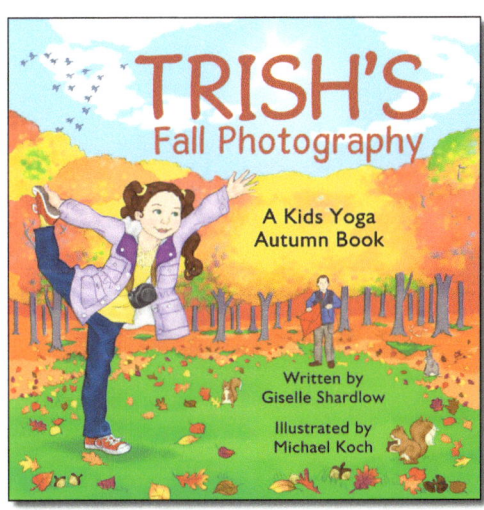

SEPTEMBER

FALL YOGA
FOCUS BREATH:
Flying Bird Breath

To practice flying bird breath, come to standing comfortably in Mountain Pose. Close your eyes if that feels comfortable or gaze gently down in front of you. Take a few deep breaths to calm your mind and body. Come to the present moment. Breathe in and out through your nose with your mouth closed.

Imagine being a bird flying through the sky. On your next inhale, lift your arms over your head, touching your palms together. Then as you exhale, bring your arms back down to your sides, touching your palms to your outer thighs.

Continue this flow for a few minutes: arms up as you inhale, arms down as you exhale. When you are ready, come back to Mountain Pose, open your eyes, and breathe naturally.

Practicing the flying bird breath is a great opportunity to combine breath and movement. Children use their bodies to pretend to fly like a bird and sync their breaths with the movement.

This breathing technique can be found in the Yoga 4 Classrooms card deck.

KIDS YOGA STORIES™
Learn. • Be Active. • Have Fun.

FALL YOGA

SEPTEMBER

FOCUS YOGA FLOW:
Warrior 3 Pose, Squat Pose, and Child's Pose

WARRIOR 3 POSE
Pretend to be a bird flying south for the winter.
Start by standing tall in Mountain Pose. Then shift your weight to stand on one leg. On an inhale, slowly bend your torso forward and squeeze your shoulder blades together while extending your arms and the other leg behind you. Gaze at the floor in front of your foot. Flex your foot so that your toes are pointing at the ground. Elongate your neck and straighten your spine so that a straight line runs from your head to your foot. Ensure that your hips are parallel to the ground. Take your arms out to the side and flap them like wings. Pretend to be a bird. Come out of the pose on an exhale, lowering your leg to the ground. Take a few deep breaths. Switch sides and repeat the steps.

SQUAT POSE
Pretend to be a squirrel collecting acorns.
Come down to a squat and pretend to be a squirrel collecting acorns.

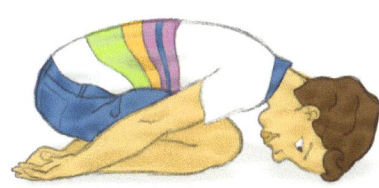

CHILD'S POSE
Pretend to be a pumpkin in a pumpkin patch.
Sit back on your heels, slowly bring your forehead down to rest in front of your knees, rest your arms down alongside your body, and take a few deep breaths. Pretend to be a pumpkin in the field.

KIDS YOGA STORIES™
Learn. • Be Active. • Have Fun.

SEPTEMBER

FALL YOGA

FOCUS YOGA BOOK:
Trish's Fall Photography

Trish's Fall Photography takes place in New England, where people from all over the world visit during the fall season to see the colorful trees, pick apples, attend fall festivals, and eat apple cider donuts. This story follows Trish and her father as they travel around their neighborhood, taking pictures of the signs of fall. Readers will act like a tree, kite, and pumpkin as they learn about fall.

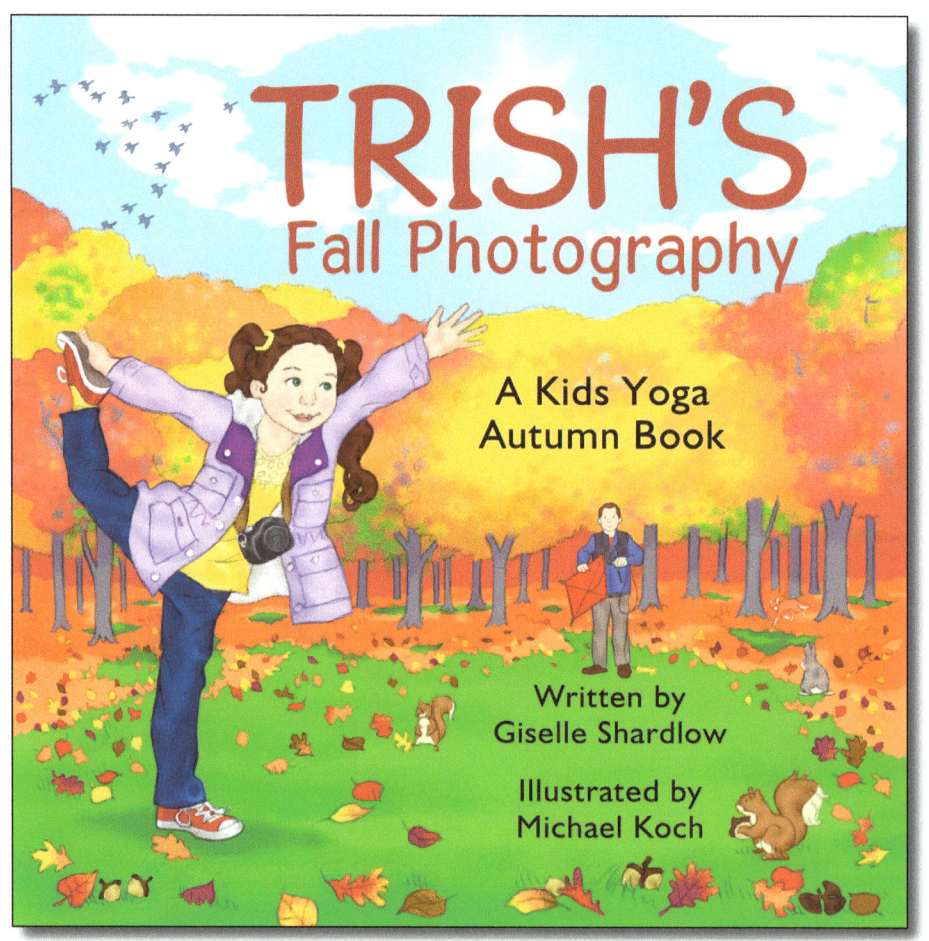

KIDS YOGA STORIES™
Learn. • Be Active. • Have Fun.

FARM YOGA

OCTOBER

Focus Breath

Bee Breath

Focus Yoga Pose

Cow Pose

Focus Yoga Flow

Cow Pose

Cat Pose

Three-Legged Dog Pose

Focus Yoga Book

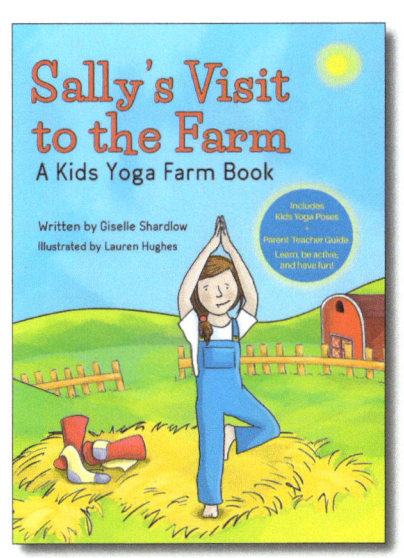

OCTOBER

FARM YOGA

FOCUS BREATH: Bee Breath

To practice bee breath, come to sitting comfortably with a tall spine and your shoulders back. Close your eyes or gaze gently down in front of you.

Take a few deep breaths to calm your mind and body. Come to the present moment. Breathe in and out through your nose with your mouth closed.

As you exhale, keep your mouth closed and make a long "mmm" sound, pretending to buzz like a bee. Then inhale through your nose, keeping your mouth closed.

Repeat the bee humming sound on the next exhale. Continue in this way with an extended inhale, followed by a humming exhale for a few minutes or as long as it feels comfortable.

When you are ready, open your eyes and breathe naturally. Notice if you feel any differently after practicing bee breath.

KIDS YOGA STORIES™
Learn. • Be Active. • Have Fun.

FARM YOGA

OCTOBER

FOCUS YOGA FLOW:
Cow Pose, Cat Pose, and Three-Legged Dog Pose

COW POSE
Pretend to be a cow about to get milked.
Come down to an all-fours position. Check that your hips are over your knees and your shoulders are over your wrists. Spread your fingers wide and flatten your palms. On an inhale, look up, arch your back, and open your chest. Moo like a cow.

CAT POSE
Pretend to be a sheep munching on hay.
As you exhale, drop your head, round your back, and tuck your chin into your chest. Pretend to be a baaing sheep. Repeat the Cow – Cat yoga pose flow a few times to awaken your spine.

THREE-LEGGED DOG POSE
Pretend to be a pony excited about getting groomed.
From an all-fours position, lift your knees, straighten your legs, and send your buttocks up into an upside-down V shape. Gently lift one leg up at a time, pretending to kick like a pony.

KIDS YOGA STORIES™
Learn. • Be Active. • Have Fun.

OCTOBER

SUMMER YOGA

FOCUS YOGA BOOK:
Sally's Visit to the Farm

Sally's Visit to the Farm follows a girl named Sally and her friend, Sam, as they tour a farm together, visiting all of the animals. Readers will act like a chicken, cow, and cat as they learn about farm animals. This book is aimed at preschoolers and kindergarteners, ages three to six.

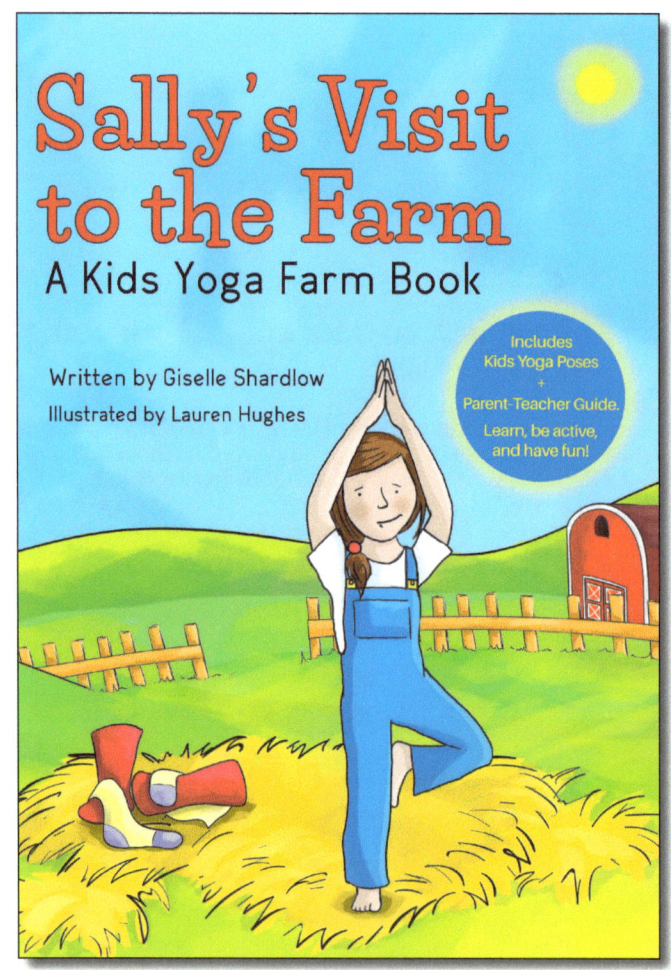

KIDS YOGA STORIES™
Learn. • Be Active. • Have Fun.

GRATITUDE YOGA

NOVEMBER

Focus Breath

Deep Belly Breath

Focus Yoga Pose

Child's Pose

Focus Yoga Flow

Child's Pose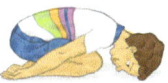

Hero Pose

Kneeling

Focus Yoga Book

NOVEMBER

GRATITUDE YOGA
FOCUS BREATH:
Deep Belly Breath

Choose a comfortable upright position such as sitting in a chair, sitting cross-legged, or sitting on your heels.

Place your right hand on your belly and your left hand on your chest. Take a deep breath in for four counts then exhale through your nose for four counts, with your lips closed. Feel the rise and fall of your chest and belly.

Do this deep belly breathing for a few minutes. Give your child a few times to get comfortable with this style of breathing.

You could use a Hoberman sphere as a visual cue to show your children the inhaling and exhaling action.

Children can think of different things that they are grateful for during each inhale and exhale.

KIDS YOGA STORIES™
Learn. • Be Active. • Have Fun.

GRATITUDE YOGA

FOCUS YOGA FLOW:
Child's Pose, Hero Pose, and Kneeling

NOVEMBER

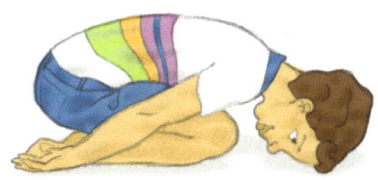

CHILD'S POSE
Pretend to be a seed.
From all-fours, come back to resting on your heels, with your arms stretched out in front of you and palms flat on the ground. Gently bring your forehead to rest on the ground in front of your knees and lay your chest on your thighs. Slowly bring your arms to rest back alongside your body. Take a few deep breaths. Pretend to be a seed planted in the earth.

HERO POSE
Pretend to be a plant.
Come back to rest upright on your heels and pretend that you are the stem of the growing plant.

KNEELING
Pretend to be a flower.
Stand on your knees, open your chest, look up, and reach up. Pretend to be a blooming flower.

KIDS YOGA STORIES™
Learn. • Be Active. • Have Fun.

NOVEMBER

GRATITUDE YOGA

FOCUS YOGA BOOK:
Hello, Bali: An Island Adventure Yoga Book

As you talk about family holidays, join one of the Yoga Kids, Anamika, and her family on their vacation around Indonesia. Say good day to this magical island through these energizing yoga poses for kids as you pretend to be a surfer, a Balinese dancer, and a monkey. Included in this island-adventure yoga book is a list of kids yoga poses, basic Indonesian phrases, and a parent-teacher guide with tips on creating a successful yoga experience. The book is aimed at toddlers and preschoolers, ages two to five.

KIDS YOGA STORIES™
Learn. • Be Active. • Have Fun.

DECEMBER

KINDNESS YOGA

Focus Breath

Balloon Breath

Focus Yoga Pose

Tree Pose

Focus Yoga Flow

Mountain Pose

Warrior 2 Pose

Tree Pose

Focus Yoga Book

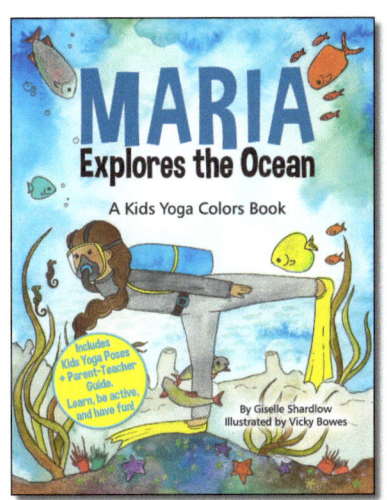

DECEMBER

KINDNESS YOGA
FOCUS BREATH:
Balloon Breath

Choose a comfortable upright position such as sitting in a chair, sitting cross-legged, or sitting on your heels. Place your hands on both knees, with palms facing up.

Open your chest and straighten your spine. Take a deep breath in for three counts while raising your arms to form the shape of a balloon. Then exhale through your nose for three counts, with your lips closed, while taking your hands back to rest on your knees.

Feel the rise and fall of your chest and belly as you continue to raise and lower your arms like a balloon inflating and deflating.

Do this balloon breathing for a few minutes. Give your child a few times to get comfortable with this style of breathing.

Your children could hold a Hoberman sphere as a visual cue to imagine the balloon inflating and deflating with their breath.

Ask the children to think of different ways to show kindness during each inhale and exhale.

KIDS YOGA STORIES™

Learn. • Be Active. • Have Fun.

KINDNESS YOGA

FOCUS YOGA FLOW:
Mountain Pose, Warrior 2 Pose, and Tree Pose

MOUNTAIN POSE
Think of being kind to yourself.
Stand tall with legs hip-width apart, feet facing forward, and take your hands together in front of you in a prayer position. Close your eyes if that's comfortable and think of being kind to yourself.

WARRIOR 2 POSE
Think of being kind to others.
From standing position, step one foot back, placing the foot so that it is facing slightly outward. Take your arms up until they are parallel to the ground, bend your front knee, and look forward. Pretend to be a "kindness warrior" being kind to others.

TREE POSE
Think of being kind to the environment.
Stand on one leg, bend your knee, place the sole of your foot on your inner thigh (or shin or ankle, but not your knee), and balance. Pretend to be a tree swaying in the breeze.

DECEMBER

KINDNESS YOGA

FOCUS YOGA BOOK:
Maria Explores the Ocean

In this story, readers act out various ocean animals native to the Pacific Ocean. The story follows a girl and her grandfather on their imaginary ocean journey. You'll also learn the chakra colors throughout the book, with a different chakra color associated with each ocean animal. This book is aimed at toddlers and preschoolers, ages two to five.

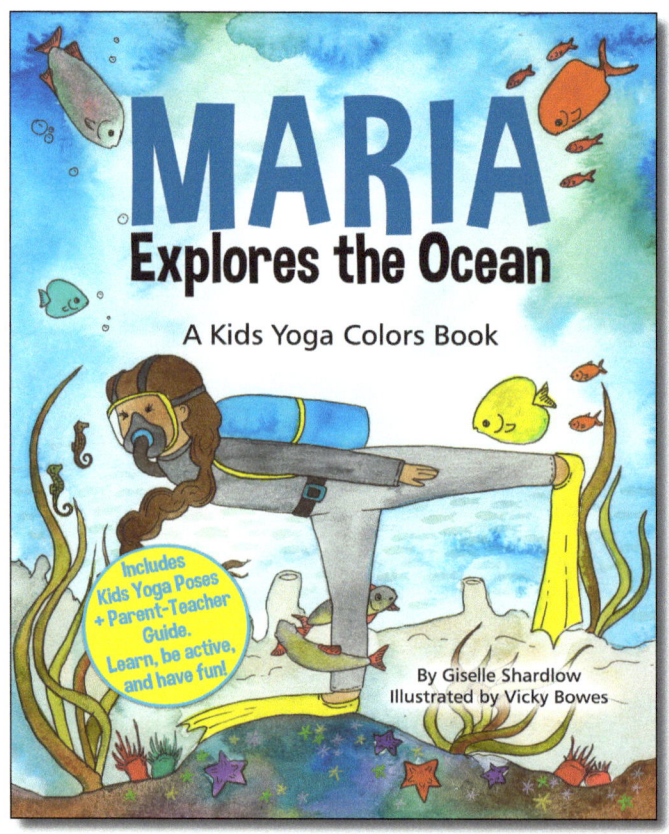

KIDS YOGA STORIES™
Learn. • Be Active. • Have Fun.

ABOUT THE AUTHOR

Giselle Shardlow draws from her experiences as a teacher, traveler, mother, and yogi to write her yoga stories for kids. The purpose of her yoga books is to foster happy, healthy, and globally educated children. She lives in Boston with her husband and daughter.

ABOUT KIDS YOGA STORIES

We hope you enjoyed your Kids Yoga Stories experience.

Visit www.kidsyogastories.com to:

RECEIVE UPDATES. For updates, contest giveaways, articles, and activity ideas, sign up for our free Kids Yoga Stories Newsletter.

CONNECT WITH US. Please share with us about your yoga journey. Send pictures of yourself practicing the poses or reading the story. Describe your journey on our social media pages (Facebook, Pinterest, Google+, and Twitter).

CHECK OUT FREE STUFF. Read our articles on books, yoga, parenting, and travel. Download one of our kids yoga lesson plans or coloring pages.

READ OR WRITE A REVIEW. Read what others have to say about our yoga stories or post your own review on Amazon or on our website. We would love to hear how you enjoyed this yoga book.

Thank you for your support in spreading our message of integrating learning, movement, and fun.

Giselle

Kids Yoga Stories
www.kidsyogastories.com
giselle@kidsyogastories.com
www.pinterest.com/kidsyogastories
www.facebook.com/kidsyogastories
www.twitter.com/kidsyogastories
www.amazon.com/author/giselleshardlow
www.goodreads.com/giselleshardlow

OTHER YOGA STORIES BY GISELLE SHARDLOW

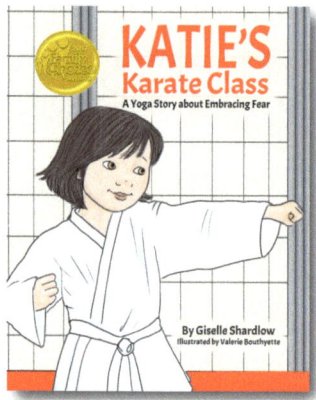 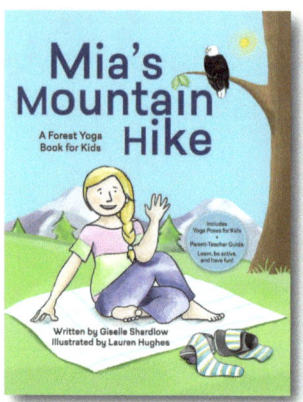 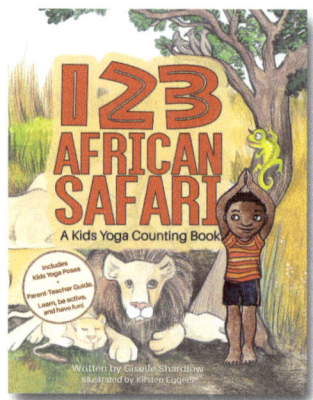

Katie's Karate Class   Mia's Mountain Hike   123 African Safari

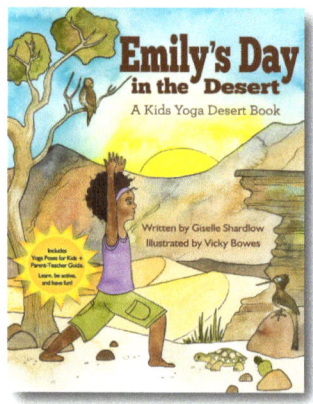 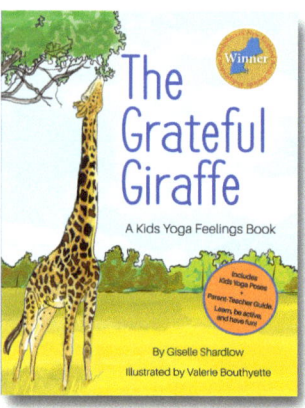 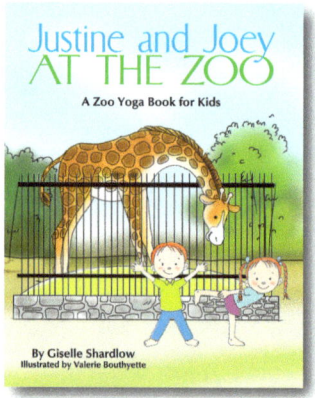

Emily's Day in the Desert   The Grateful Giraffe   Justine and Joey at the Zoo

Kids Yoga Class Ideas

www.kidsyogastories.com

www.ingramcontent.com/pod-product-compliance
Lightning Source LLC
LaVergne TN
LVHW072126070426
835512LV00002B/20